Toys Tune In

Published by Scholastic Inc., Publishers since 1920. SCHOLASTIC and associated logos
are trademarks and/or registered trademarks of Scholastic Inc. All rights reserved.

The publisher does not have any control over and does not assume
any responsibility for author or third-party websites or their content.

ISBN: 978-1-338-57293-3

10 9 8 7 6 5 4 3 2 1   19 20 21 22 23

Printed in Malaysia   106

First printing, 2019

Book design by Marissa Asuncion

Scholastic Inc.

Woody and the other toys got **used** to watching TV when Andy was home sick. They had a great **view** from Andy's bed.

"What do you want to watch?" asks Bo Peep.

Rex, the dinosaur, wants to watch a show about a **huge** reptile.

"That reptile is very scary," says Rex.

Hamm, the piggy bank, wants to watch a show about a superhero.

"This superhero can save the **universe**," says Hamm.

The Green Army Men
want to watch a show
about an army **unit**.

"Keep an eye out for green **uniforms**," says Sarge. "Or listen for a **bugle** call."

Buzz and the aliens
want to watch a show
about space.
Buzz takes the remote control.

"I saw a space show
back there," says Buzz.
"All I need to do is figure out
which button to **use**."

Buzz hits a **few** buttons.
Then he hits the **volume** button.
Sound blasts from the TV!

Bo Peep **uses** her staff
to hit the **mute** button.
She turns down the sound.

"That's much better," she says.

Woody wants all the toys
to agree on one show.

"Let's not **argue**," he says.
"What do we all want to watch?"

"Something **cute**,"
says Bo Peep.

"A **musical**!" says Jessie.

Then right on **cue**,
a voice from the TV says,
"Stay tuned for *Woody's
Roundup*!"

The toys settle down
to watch TV.
And they make sure
Woody has the best **view** of all.